Feels Like Tuesday

An anthology of words and thoughts of a working class Black man

Feels Like Tuesday

Copyright © 2021 by Blue Collah

No part of this book may be used or reproduced in any manner whatsoever without the prior written permission of the author and artist.

This book is dedicated to...

To anybody that's waiting on the right time or feeling . To anyone that thinks they're not skilled enough...hopefully this will inspire you to get out of your own way. Your skill is influenced by your experiences. Your experiences are all the training you need.
No matter what age, or background, it's never too late.

Don't be afraid to put it on paper. Create.

Last but definitely not least: To all the Atlanta Public School teachers that inspired me as a youth, Thank You.

In Peace,

-Blue Collah

Introduction

I created this book for the days that you have nothing planned on your calendar. It seems like Tuesday is the one day you can define as your own. This piece of work is the product of the collaboration of a brilliant Atlanta Artist, Vernon Robinson Sr. Vernon, thank you , not only for your much needed encouragement but also being my brother in truth, love, and Christ.

-Blue Collah

Could You Be Jazz?

Could you be Jazz?
Complex, rhythmic, soulful all at once.
Your seduction so subtle yet accomplished without even a touch;
Warmth and cool intermingled; whatever the moment calls for.
Motion fluid with no interruption.
Hidden passion not easily captured; not on canvas , not with words.
Yet it's so easy to become engulfed in your music.

Urban Go-Real-ah

Sometimes you get caught up in somethangs, some thangs some thangs... This city life, spending money, spending money. But them magazines, them videos, them uptown Hustlers say that's what it's all about.

 The car, them clothes, that crib... You supposed to have it all. Them Hustlers said that Saturn you drivin' cramps your style.

How nasty them chitlins was on Thanksgiving? And guess what, the pig ear is probably one that fell out of Pooky's daddy boot from 68; when the restaurant was a packed house. The HUSTLE? $300,000 for a "condo" that you know twenty years ago was an apartment renting for $700 a month. But that's what it's all about in the city. Who pimpin who? Yeah but you like it... make you feel like you belong, don't you feel GOOD!!! You've arrived!

Thoughts from the Left

kickin' it to the left

A warm wind blowing from the west touches my face; an evening breeze not yet cooled by the cover of the coming night.
A breeze capturing your fragrance imprinted upon it. To ride into your wind blowing from the west; your wind with small particles of desert sand blowing about, how inviting as I ride; trying to catch the sun before it sets on you. Yet if I cannot outrun the darkness, your breeze will keep me warm throughout the night.

All the Above

The sound of a train at 3 o'clock in the morning as you lay awake with sleep no where to be found, eyes fixed on the dark but looking for the light.
Hands waiting for touch that might not be there, heart longing for the rhythm and beat of another to relate to.
It might not come.
Ah, but the train, I can always get the train to take me there.
There's just something about the train
It sounds good no matter how far away, just as long as you can hear it.
That train plays any kind of music you wanna hear.
Funk, jazz, blues, gospel.
Brook heard it in Georgia while it was raining. You can take it home in the morning because the one in the evening might be too late. Duke took the "A".
When all else fails, that train, that train baby will take you where you want to go.

Vibes

I lay here listening to the saxophone play you all night.
Capturing your motion, your stillness.
Capturing your high notes, your low notes.
There is no escaping you tonight.
Surrounded by vibration so unique, so untypical , so you, only you.
As I lay here, as flow becomes vibe, as vibe becomes touch
Can every night be like this?

Age of Arrogance

How did we arrive at this point?
It has become apparent that the majority of people in our nation have no voice. In the past it seems someone or some group would always remind the people of power that the workers are the true stakeholders and decide whether the country fails or succeeds.

...Late to the game

Playing ball during the day
Harlem at night
Ella...Duke... Count...Billie at night
Beautiful women, food cooked by the best
Vibrations other people have to orchestrate... always have been... always will be...
What makes the water cold?
Farm to table...that bright red tomato, cucumbers, squash as bright as the sun
Granddaddy's gardens 50 years ago
Taken for granted
Little did u know everybody else was late to the game
Ya'll hate...
Sometimes u get caught
Money is not what makes it taste good, sound good
The people with money are always

late to the game
U get to experience it first
Everything grows from the ground up
Your art, your music, your food, your talent
You don't need validation
You are great. You are already valid
The people with money are always late to the game
Your greatness does not come from the people
People destroy history, burn books.
Basquiat's Art...brilliance
Basquiat was brilliant before it ever was placed in a mansion in Malibu, a museum in Milan
U got to see it on the streets, knew it was great then...Money
Always late to the game
Jazz, Blues, Hip Hop, Gospel,
Mays, Aaron, Robinson, Satch
We saw them FIRST
Greatness

Money always late to the game
They always gonna be late
Cannot wait for the money, know you are great
Do what U DO.
Trust YOUR intellect
Let no one define U but U
If it's good, it's good
No explanation needed
A guess is a guess even if its educated.
How many times do you have to go around the same circle?

Mr. Floyd

My Blackness won't let me sleep
We have seen it before... we have been warned.
Nothing new. Voices that we heard still relevant.
Voices that we should have groomed our children to hear.
These voices we should have made an inheritance.
In a time like this, we knew Mr. Floyd's murder was going to happen.
America was groomed for it.
Marvin Gaye hollered about it.
Gil Scott got us ready for it.
Lonnie Jordan.
Last Poets
So relevant . Aint nothing new.
We slept...Our children were not introduced to the voices.
Listen with them and let them know this was nothing unpredictable.
America has been headed in this direction forever.

Yet do not be discouraged or tired. The fight will continue.
There will always be a fight.
There will always be a challenge.
Mr. Floyd challenged us.
His murder should never be forgotten.
Sleep comes when it comes.
Don't waste the time you have.
Being woke is not enough.
Your eyes are open NOW.
Stretch... take a deep breath for Mr. Floyd.
 Fill your lungs.
Trust me, you will need it.
This marathon has no end in sight but you are not running alone.
Sometimes it might feel like it.
Too many people have made it before you were here.
Run toward the future, trust me some will be there to take over.
Mr. Floyd deserves our endurance.
Git down with the git gown.
Make it do what it do. Coming out of the toughness and into the roughness.

He spoke to us in his silence.
Lying in the street.
But what he was saying was heard all through the universe.
Still echoing...It will echo forever in me.
My Blackness won't let it leave.
Mr. Floyd's death is keeping me alive.
Alive to challenge this injustice .
This injustice that is as American as America.

Go Deep (skin diver)

Do you see me? I see you
 see your smile, your warmth, maybe your
cold, your calm
But my look tries to go beyond your surface
Will you please do the same for me?
Is it that you are afraid? Or could it be that
if you look long enough you might see something that attracts you.
Could it be that if you look beyond my physical self you may be awakened to see my true self? My spirit?
But you have to trust yourself to see it
These scars, these scars are just a reminder of my history.
 A deep line of beautiful people with scars
We all have them. Some you can see. Some you cannot.
That scar on your heart, your hand, your face means that you are healing
That scar means that you have been through some things but you made it
That scar, no matter how big, wear it proud

Let it show so that others will know they can live through it
No matter the situation

Mall Walk

I see you, them tattoos you got peeking out from certain places on your skin
Them tattoos ducking and hiding and disappearing into them tight places
You look good but it ain't the tattoos, it's you.
It's those brown eyes peeking from behind those designer sun glasses.
It's those big juicy lips that don't need injections, it's those hips that you couldn't hide even if you wanted to... don't hide'em.
It all makes you, you.
You are unique, those eye, those lips, those hips.
Don't let'em trick you, they all wanna be like you

Weeks End

Sometimes words don't come easy
Looking for a vibe, searching for a groove best found without being chemically induced
A Friday night thang
So unBlack to be searching on a Friday night
Friday night, everything oughta be in place
Clothes, money, love
Friday night, everything flows
Just flow with it
Time to fly!!
Land softly.

Subjects

Subjects of the heart need not be explained.

Sometimes the best love is left unmade.

Put it On Paper...

There is just something about a "BOOK"
I find writing in long hand for me is just better.
Maybe it's because I enjoy the quietness of the pen as it touches the paper.
Or it could be that I enjoy that every stroke on paper is "your art only"
Not transformed by machinery or automation.

Rain in Houston

Rainy nights are meant to be shared. A
great excuse for dreamers
A great excuse for lovers sometimes water
makes things go down easier

Interruptions

Loneliness interrupted by thoughts of you are interruptions quite welcomed.

Stereotypes

Spending your life running from stereotypes
Spent most of your life running from
stereotypes, finally realizing we all fit the
profile.
Change your hair, change your clothes,
change your "money"
But the rules never change
Oh no, don't order that chicken, THEY might
mistake you for one of THEM
Almond roasted salmon please

The Trust I Extend

The trust extended to you cannot be folded up and put away as if it were cash placed back in a pocket, not like a carpenter's retractable ruler.
The trust extended to you is there more for me than for you.
Th trust extended for you cannot be placed back inside my heart
The trust extended to you cannot be reversed.
The trust extended to you whether used or unused, I have no right to take it back.
The trust extended... hopefully you can find refuge in at times

Fittin' In

As a people we spend so much time trying to figure out how we fit into the "human equation".

It's very simple.

You are the equation in its entirety.

Bittersweet

This love I share cannot be filtered.
The sweet must be enjoyed along with the bitter.
One is no good without the other.

Mouth to Mouth

Reaching for light, only grabbing air; air that cannot be ingested or digested, only breathed

Cleansing not only lungs but thoughts as well

Air is to be shared unselfishly

Air is better when it is shared

Blown into a distressful situation can be quite welcomed

Air not sterile

But with organisms of love and all that comes with it

Matter so small it does not catch the eye but can be seen only by the heart

Music for One

The distance between us is needed.

Its best to find ourselves before we find each other.

Water

Your water so cool when thirsts need quenching and warm when the situation calls.
Your water quenches the thirst of so many who need a drink.
Your water flows with calm that is soothing to the spirit.
Your water brings life to situations that may have needed nourishment.
Your water so cool yet warm to the touch.
The wetness of water, there is nothing else like it.
Black woman, I thank you for sharing your spiritual water.
If I were stranded on the desert I can think of no one better to share a drink with than you.

Touch

The art of oneness is unexplainable to those who have never experienced it.
Sharing a heartbeat, an emotion, a soft touch not hand made nor man made.
A touch not measured by time but you wish it could last forever.
A touch so much more gratifying than physical.

Billion Dollar Groove

Sad to say flow is something that doesn't come with a price.
The city is trying so hard to find itself.
Looking so hard for something that's already here.

Connection

Sometimes it's so hard trying to connect all of the dots in our day to day lives. I guess because it seems there are so many of them to connect.

Maybe we try too hard. Maybe we make things more complex than they really are. I know I do that at times.

So much stuff in front of us, we don't know what to tackle first. But one thing is for certain...

If we are patient, God will connect all of our dots for us!

Just felt the need to talk...enjoy your day whether sun or rain.

Bourgeois Up Boogie Down

Sometimes you have to bring your nose down to life's level to smell what's going on around you.

It might be pleasant, it might be unpleasant but it will keep you alive and experiencing things you've missed as you've tried to go through life holding your breath.
Afraid to breathe.

Things grow from the ground up.
Don't limit your self to pleasure...
You will become numb to the things that really matter.
Spiritual growth, family, friends, helping others.
With a nose in the clouds you cannot smell when you are needed.

Outside the Box

Opening up to a thought process, no planning involved.
Unguided by a destination.
Following something bigger than me.
On a faith journey...Liberating...
My responsibility is just starting the trip.

I Can't Breathe

"I cannot breathe".
It took a man being choked to death.
The air that he was denied that day
resuscitated an entire country. Hopefully
"we" have started to breathe again. Using
his air, this precious life to stand up and
speak out, and act upon the injustice that
we face.
I do not think he realized it but that day Eric
Garner gave America mouth to mouth.
Let us not waste his gift of life to us.
"I have a dream", on a balcony in Memphis.
Dr. King succumbed to an assassins bullet.
His blood being shed. Blood that we should
use as a transfusion. A transfusion to give
us the energy to fight a little while longer.
The courage to face the challenges of
today.
Air denied, blood lost.

This should be a reminder to us. We are here for a purpose. Let us not forget those who have sacrificed their lives so that we might enjoy freedom.

Yet as we believers all know who gave the ultimate sacrifice many years ago.

Nailed to a cross.

This ultimate sacrifice charges us to love and lift up our fellow brothers and sisters. As we move forward let us not take this charge that we have lightly.

Ms. Interpret

If I saw your tattoo...No not that one... you know the one you try to hide...that one that's only visible when you truly trust for it to be viewed.
You keep it deep. That's ok.
It's not for everyone. Not to be shown on every occasion.
It's cool when you want it to be cool.
Sometimes it's fire red hot...out of control hot... burning you from inside out.
A good fire you cannot keep just for yourself.
A flame to share. But everyone can't be trusted with fire...
Yeah... some tattoos are best to keep close to you. Kept in the heart... can't let everyone in...might be too hot...might be misinterpreted...

...beauty is in the eye of the beautiful...
Thank you for letting me inside...can tell by your a
not too many have experienced it.
I am honored to be here.
Hopefully I can linger...

No Rules of Engagement

Let love go.
Trying to hold on to a feeling that makes
sense. That rope slowly slipping out of my
hand, pulling me to the other side, trying to
resist the thought of being fulfilled.
No rush, no hurry, making my own music.
Thank you for engaging me in such a
wonderful back and forth.
You never play fair.
Your advantages are too many to count.
You use them all.

Escape

Reading allows you to create your own air and atmosphere.
Define the subject in your own terms.
Reading gives you a chance to see things and experience situations that you may never experience physically.

Cover art title :
Third World Canvas
by: Vernon Robinson Sr.

Photo Credit Back Cover: Keith Jackson

Made in the USA
Columbia, SC
13 February 2025